Hurt

Poetry by Nicola Ward

Published 2012 by Lulu Press
3101 Hillsborough St.
Raleigh, NC 27607

Printed in the United States of America

ISBN: 978-1-4452-2806-8

Hurt

To Mam and Dad with love…

Table of Contents

The Intruder

Every night she's scared to try sleep
Her once favourite place has become a place of fear
Where all her worst nightmares come true night after night
And she must endure it without shedding a tear

She lies in the dark waiting for the sound
Knowing the intruder is lurking around
Waiting until everyone else is asleep
So there's no one to hear her scream
And tell her it's just a dream

First come the names and all her faults
"You're ugly, you're stupid, you're fat"
"You're hopeless, everyone hates you, you should die"
There's no one to convince her it's a lie

Then comes the pain, followed by the blood
While the names and laughter continue to flood
Flooding her mind and she cannot fight
Deep down inside she knows they're right

Finally the intruder gets bored with its prey
It leaves her alone until the next day
Calmness overtakes her but she knows it won't last
For the intruder is herself, the intruder is her past

Painful Secrets

Painful secrets, shameful past
Relive the hurt of days gone past
Blocked out for so long
The only way I could carry on

But now it's back and I suffer again
Just as I did way back then
If I find the strength to face it now
It may help heal the hurt, somehow

Why Mammy?

The little girl lies in bed, but really lies inside her head
Watching herself cry endless tears, why mammy why?

She clutches her teddy tight, the only friend she can trust
Everyone else hurts her, even those who say they love her

Who can she trust in this lonely cruel world?
Left alone in pain and tears night after night

And they say they hurt her because they love her
But how could that be?

As the tears dry she regains her focus
And sees herself as she is from outside

Not a child but a grown up woman
So why is she still a child inside?

Why did they rob her of her innocence and dreams?
Why mammy why?

How Was I to Know?

That "I want to protect you"
Meant you want to hurt me
That "I'll always love you"
Meant until someone else came along
That "we'll be together forever"
Meant until you'd no further use for me
That "I'm not like other guys"
Meant you're even worse
That "I'll never make you cry"
Meant you wouldn't want to know
That "I'd do anything for you"
Meant anything to hurt me
That "you're the one I love"
Meant there's someone else
How was I to know that everything (I thought) we had
Was just a lie

The Broken Child

The broken child picks herself up
With the help of those around her (and herself)
She begins to put the pieces back together
Slowly but surely, so they will stay

Beginning to trust, learning to love again
Seeing that maybe she's not completely bad
Letting go of regrets and pain
Knowing they led to her destiny
And her happiness

And all the pain in her world is replaced by beauty
It was there all along
She had only to open her eyes to see it

Friend

Sometimes when I'm blue
I stop and think of you
Suddenly the world is a better place
I have a smile on my face
Because you're my friend
Until the end
You make my life complete
I hope I can make you happy too
If you're ever blue

Scars

You've got scars, I'm alarmed
You've got scars, all over your arms
You've got tears on your face
I've got tears, you're all over the place

I want to love you
I want to need you
But you push me away
Nothing to say

You've got scars, I'm alarmed
You've got scars, all over your arms
I see blood, on your wrist
You see hurt, I'm in a twist

I want to love you
I want to need you
I see pain in your eyes
You see hope in mine

I see it in your eyes
I see it in your eyes
The pain you feel inside

I want to love you
I want to need you you'll get through this one day
I'll show you the way

Ed (Eating Disorder)

I need you but I don't want to
I love you but I hate you
You're everything but you leave me with nothing
I want to let you go
But you hold on so
Without you I'm nothing
But what am I with you?
Only broken and sad

I'll never be thin enough for you
Yet I still try to please you
You always demand more
All I get is grief
You'll kill me before you'll see me happy
You just won't go away
Well I'll fight you everyday
To get my life back

Cos I'm worth more than anything
You give me
I get more from my loved ones
Then you make me lie to them
Well I won't listen anymore
But I don't know if I can stop
I'm torn between you and recovery
But how can I do that to everyone?
Let you take my life from me
I will be good, but at recovery
I'll live a normal life and make people proud
And not because I'm thin
Where will you be then?
I really don't care
Just leave me alone
It's your turn to suffer

Suicide

Dear Friend
If you could pass me a razor
Cos my wrists are calling out
Begging me to end my life
Bury me in black
Let me kiss you before I go

But I can't do this because I can't leave you

Now turn away
Cos I'm awful to see
The blood all over my body
The pain is agony
Won't you help me baby
Part of me wants to go

But I can't do this because I can't leave you

Please don't ever say goodbye
Because I would cry

But I can't do this because I can't leave you

True Beauty

Being thin isn't everything
Success and beauty don't equal being thin
Success is happiness
Real beauty comes from within
There's no such thing as perfect
Eating disorders have so many bad effects
So don't feel you must be thin
Just to fit in
The people who really care
Will see true beauty is there
In the person you are inside
Not who you are outside

Thin

A girl so thin
With burns on her skin
Bandages on her wrists
No weight on her hips
Eyes so sad
Is it so bad
That you want to die
Can you tell me why
All I can say
Is for you I will pray

Act

All day long I put on an act
Fine, good, happy go lucky
But when I'm alone I begin to crack
Everyone loves me when I'm funny
But who'll be there when the laughter stops
I try to cry and I plan how to die
Nobody knows, they think I'm fine
They don't know I'm just good at lying
Keep them laughing and they'll never know
That I'm crying and screaming inside
The part of me I always hide
Who'll see the scars or feel the hunger but me
Too busy to notice, too busy to care
I try to ask for help but there's no one there

Reality

She hides in the shadows
Afraid of what's outside
She can't accept reality
So she lives inside her mind

No one bothers her there
She can be who she wants
At least that's how it started
Now she's scared there too

She flees from one to the other
Desperately trying to feel safe
But she's trapped between two worlds
Like a restless spirit trying to break free

Mask

I put on some make up
And I hide behind a mask
No one knows how I feel
And no one bothers to ask
I smile all day long
So no one knows anything is wrong
I keep up a happy face
No one knows I'm all over the place
But at the end of the day
When the mask comes off
I break down and cry
I don't even know why

Ed 2

Constantly lightheaded
I walk around half dead
All because of my fear
Which began here
When you called me fat
Why did you do that

Now I'm stuck in hell
But no one can tell
Cos I'm not thin enough yet
But you can bet
That one day I will be
What's happening to me

Why am I doing this to myself
Why will no one help
I just want to be free
But I'm scared of me
I could kill myself doing this
But the voice continues to hiss

And so I obey
I will make it happy one day
For now I just feel sad
How did things get so bad
When will enough be enough
Why is the voice so tough
I'm scared but I can't stop

Self Harm

I can't say what I want to say
So I say it in another way
By drawing a blade across my wrist
Shows the world I'm in a twist
But I don't show it to anyone
That wouldn't be fun

They'd think I was a freak
Who can't just speak
About what's troubling me
But they don't see
How hard it is for me to express
When I cut myself it's like a test

Can I take the pain
And will I gain
Some sense of control
Like I had before
When I could cope
Before I lose all hope
Now I take it back again
I feel no pain

Just a sense of relief
Instead of my grief
Now I'm free to carry on
To the world I am strong
Although I have scars on my skin
The real scars are within

Ed 3

I step on the scales and frown
Why aren't the numbers going down
I ate an extra apple today
I'll never lose weight that way
Always listen to the voice
I no longer have a choice
One day I'll be thin
But I'll pay for my sins
I'll be sick as well
My life will be hell
I'll throw it all away
Just to be thin one day
Is it really worth this mess
Should I keep eating less
Will I die before I get there
Will I even care
As long as I am thin
Then I can begin
To feel happy inside
For now I must hide
How little I eat
Food takes a backseat
To the voice in my head
That wants me dead
I'm not strong enough to fight
I know it must be right
When it says not to eat anymore
Why can't I show it the door
And take my life back
Get off this track
Before it's too late
Oh how I hate
What I put myself through
Just to please you
Stupid voice in my head
It's time YOU were dead

Escape

Wanting to escape
But I don't know how
All I know is to bleed and starve
Sick of feeling so low
Why can't I get away
From the thing inside my head
Taunting and mocking me
As I lie in bed
Wanting to be saved
But I have to save myself
Or I'll be lying in a grave
Where will my soul be then
Down in hell paying for my sins
Or up in heaven

Will I ever get away from myself
Or am I stuck like this forever
All I want is help
But I don't deserve it
I'm not ill enough
I caused my own problems
They're all inside my head
So why should anyone help me
I deserve to be dead

Crushed

Feeling so low because you're gone
Seems there's no pint in carrying on
I try to keep a smile on my face
But inside I'm all over the place
Abandoned by you when I needed you most
Now our love is just a ghost
Missing you so much I can't breathe
Being back with you is such a strong need
But instead all I do is bleed
Red tears I'm constantly crying
My hope you'll talk to me again is slowly dying
Now I'm just a broken mess
Who would ever have guessed
That you'd hurt me like this
I still long for your kiss
But it wasn't to be
Now there's just me
Left all alone
With a pain that keeps growing

Without You

Without you my world has stopped turning
Inside is a pain that is burning
No point in being alive
I just want to hide

Without you the world is grey
No happiness in my day
I know I must go on
But I don't know if I can be that strong

Without you I'm empty inside
All my tears I have to hide
I must keep smiling because it's expected of me
But all I want to do is scream

Without you there's no point to anything
I no longer sing
Just think of you
Which makes me feel blue

Without you a part of me has died
So many tears I have cried
Just hoping you're ok
And you'll talk to me again one day

Gone

I used to hold you in my arms
I fell for all your charms
You always made me laugh
Now all that's left is a photograph

I hold my pillow tight
Dream of you every night
I pretend you're still here
That I'm holding you near

You were only a phone call away
You brightened up every day
We had so many good times
Now I'm left crying
Thinking of you
Is all I can do
My heart is broken
So many words left unspoken

But now it's too late
You sealed out fate
When you said goodbye
I felt I would die

Poems

All these poems I'm writing for you
Are you writing them for me too
Do you ever think about me
Do you wish we had agreed
Does your heart ache
Do you think we made a mistake
Are you carrying on
Memories of me already gone
Thinking about the next one
Moving onto another love

Lonely Christmas

Finding it hard to let go
Dreaming of you in the snow
I usually love this time of year
But what's the point when you're not here
I do my shopping and try to smile
But I'm thinking of you all the while
Christmas morning will be so sad
Without you here holding my hand
I don't know if you realise how I feel
My love for you is still real
You'll probably never know how much I care
And how I wish I was there
Wherever you are now
Still with you somehow
I write these poems but I realise
You'll never get to read these lines
If you did would you care too
Or would they mean nothing to you

Heartbreak

I could write a million poems
But you wouldn't come back to me
I could cry a million tears
But you still wouldn't see
How much I love and need you
How my heart is breaking in two
Please come back
Cos I can't hack
Being without you
Life is so blue
Without you in it
I hurt every minute
Why don't you care
Why are you there
Not here with me
Happy as can be

The Price of Love

When you're in love it's great
Looking forward to the next date
But all good things come to an end
That is the truth, my friend
What are you left with but a broken heart
If you'd known that from the start
Would you still have gone out with him
Knowing you'd be left pretty grim
Do you think of good times and smile
Or are you crying a long while
Late at night when you lie in bed
Are thoughts of him running through your head
Can you forget or is it too much
Is moving on an option as such
If the price of love is hurting like this
Is it really worth it, or should you give it a miss
They say true love comes at a price
For me true love is suicide

It's Over

Now it's time I moved on
It's my turn to be strong
Sick of feeling broken hearted
As I've been since we parted
You obviously just don't care
If you did you'd still be there
But you've chosen not to be
And now I can see
There's no point trying to hold on
What we had is gone
So why should I think of you
And feel blue
If you're happy without me
I'll feel the same
No more pain
I won't think of you when I hear our song
I won't think this is all wrong
I'll forget we belonged together
I won't think of you ever

Smile

Smile though inside you're dying
Smile though you feel like crying
Never let anyone know
That you just want to go
Away from this life
And all it's strife
Keep laughing so no one will guess
You're not the best
They won't want to know

Smile even though he left you
Smile though you don't know what to do
Never let on you're hurting inside
Always keep a smile on the outside
Cos no one will care
That he's no longer there
And you're left all alone
No more calls on your phone
As long as you're smiling no one will know
As long as you're smiling they'll think you've let go

Feeling Unreal

How can I know I'm real?
I don't know how to feel
When everything around me is strange
I just want to change
Back to when I felt normal
When the world wasn't full
Of things that don't look real
What is the deal?
Why is everything suddenly unfamiliar
I don't know where I am
Or what anything is anymore
I want to feel like before
Before I felt I was losing my mind
Why can't I find
Something to make this go away
Just to feel normal everyday

Suicide 2

I'm sorry I left you
I really am
But I couldn't go on
I was stuck in a jam

Of disordered eating
And cutting myself
I didn't know how
To ask for help

So now I'm gone
But you must go on
Living your life
Without me and my strife

A life you deserve
I deserved one too
But I just couldn't cope
So I had to leave you

Ana (Anorexia)

I heard a lyric today
That ana wrecks your life
I know it's true
But I'm stuck with all this strife

I tell myself just to ear
I can't understand
Why there's no one there
To hold my hand

So instead I keep starving myself
I turn away from all their help
Because they're not him
And he is gone
He left me alone
I can't carry on

But I know that I must
For the people who care
And maybe one day
There'll be someone else there

Miss You

I miss you so much
It's killing me
Why did you leave me
I didn't want to be free

Free from your love
And all that it brang
My heart fluttering
Every time you rang

Now my phone is silent
You're no longer there
I try not to cry
I try not to care

You left me again
To deal with my pan
More hunger and scars
Upon my arms

Without You 2

Without you my world stops turning
Inside is a pain that is burning
I know I wrote this poem before
But in all honesty, you meant more

More than him
Or anyone else
I'd have done anything for you
I thought you loved me too

Without you I'm an empty shell
Yet everyone thinks I'm ding well
They don't see the pain inside
When you left I felt I had died

Maybe ana wrecks your life
But now I'll never be your wife
So what's the point
I may as well give in
Because my real scars are within

Self Harm 2

Bracelets and wristbands cover my wrists
So no one can see I'm in a twist
Cos I can't fight anymore
I want to show self harm the door

But it's always been there for me
Why can no one see?
That I'm hurting inside
Every night I cry

Because I'm all alone
No one's ringing my phone
I'm afraid to reach out
What if they just shout?

That I really am worthless and no good
That I don't deserve any food
Self harm and disordered eating are ruining my life
But I can't get out
I cannot fight

Derealisation

Sometimes when I'm walking about
I suddenly want to scream and shout
Because everything looks weird
Am I really here?

I was fine a minute ago
But now I don't know
If anything is real
Or what I feel

It's called derealisation
But I never stopped at this station
Or asked for this
Ignorance is bliss

I used to feel safe as can be
I never knew this would happen to me
I'd no longer know how normal feels
Why can't I just be real?

Scar Tattoos

My arms are covered in scar tattoos
Wouldn't you love to be in my shoes?
Crying every night
Trying so hard to fight
Exhausted from it all
Hiding behind a wall
The world doesn't seem real
Does anyone know how I feel?
I just want to die
But I hold my head high
And act like I'm fine
This "perfect" life of mine

Break Up

You understood everything I said to you
I told you I loved you
You said you loved me too
You once judged me
Or made me feel a freak
The only one with whom I could speak

Then one day out of the blue
You turned to me
And broke my heart in two
Said you couldn't be with me anymore
Then you walked out the door
Now I'm all alone and you want to be friends
But you just don't get it
I want my life to end

Family

I can't take too many pills again
Cos that would only cause you pain
You sat all night in hospital with me
How I did that to you, I still can't see

I can't slit my wrists
That would leave you in bits
And I can't cut deep
Not enough to put me to sleep

I could starve myself to death
But I'm a long way from that yet
That would hurt you too
It would make you blue

So maybe instead I'll get well
Get myself out of this hell
Why would I want to leave my family
When I know how much they love me

Regret

Looking down on you from heaven
Can't believe we're no longer seven
Seven of us in our family
Not anymore, because I killed me
Why I did it I just don't know
The pain inside just seemed to grow
Until I couldn't take it anymore
I should have tried harder to ignore

And got on with things
And the joy you bring
Now it's too late
I've sealed our fate

And left you behind
Cos I couldn't find
A reason to stay
For another day

If I'd just looked at you
I wouldn't have gone through
With ending my life
You'd have made things alright

Fighting Ed

Counting the minutes until my next meal
Why on earth do I feel
That I must obsess about food
When I'm in a low mood

Why do I worry about numbers on a scale
And will I live to tell the tell
Of a diet gone wrong
An obsession so strong

I must fight every day
Mustn't fade away
Cos I've so much to give
So many reasons to live

Love

We're so much in love
I feel like a dove
Able to fly
No need to cry

Cos you cheer me up
Without your love I'd give up
I'm so lucky to have you
I hope you love me too

Then you said you can't be with me
Well now I am free
In a dark place under the ground
My suicide note you found

How Love Feels

Will I tell you how love feels
It's that feeling of joy
When you see your boy
It's the way you light up
When he shows up
It's the way you feel
He makes you feel real
No longer depressed
You feel you're the best

Will I tell you how love feels
It's that time you waited by my side
That night I almost died
From the pills I took
When my world was shook
Cos he's no gone
I can't carry on

Alone

You left me all alone
In this cruel world
You left me crying tears
But also crying blood

But I won't let you keep me down
My heart is mine
Not yours to own
I'll be happy again with time

Texts

Why do you keep texting me
Why don't you stop
Why don't you see

That I do want you to text
But I don't
That I do want to reply
But I won't

Cos you keep hurting me
Why don't you stop
Why don't you see

That I do want you to love me
But I don't
That I do want to love you too
But I won't

Cos it's over now
You made your choice and how
Many times should I take you back
By now I've lost track
So I'm staying away you see
You can no longer hurt me

Acting

Every day I play a role
Of someone in control
Sailing through each day
Happy in every way

Every day I play a part
Of someone without a broken heart
No one sees the tears I shed
Or what goes on inside my head

Every day I follow a script
Of someone better than this
Who doesn't starve or cut herself
And isn't afraid to ask for help

Life and Death

Why is he gone and not me
How can one just cease to be
Why do I get to be alive
While he didn't survive
Am I really dead
Or messed up in the head
Why did he not wake up again
Did he feel any pain
Where is he now
Looking down on us somehow
Am I real
How would I deal
If it was someone close to me
From my family
I should just be glad
My life is still to be had

My Worst Enemy

My enemy, the voice in my head
Pretends to be my friend
Yet only wants me dead

Tells me not to eat
That I must be thin
This voice I will defeat

I will fight
Whatever it says
I know it's not right

Yes I will be saved
Whatever it takes
I won't dig my own grave

Fog in my Head

When it happens I want to hide
I'm walking through a fog
You're all on the other side

A defence gone wrong
I hate it so
I no longer sing my song

Just want to feel right
This problem I have
It gives me a fright

I don't know myself
Who I am
Or anyone else

Nightmare

A tense feeling in my body
He's on top of me again
Holding me down
Trying to suffocate me
Night after night
I try to scream
But nothing comes out
I try to push him off
But I can't move
Then I wake up
Thank God
It was just a bad dream

Red Carnage

Hidden in the shadows of night
Wondering whether to bite
Or cut her own skin
She cries within
At the red carnage caused
All because she is lost

Lost in her mind
Too scared to find
What happened in her past
She uses a razor at last
Watch the blood flow
Remember how she used to glow
Now she glows red tears
Cos she is so full of fears

No Longer Mine

You were mine
If only for a time
But like them all
You let me fall
Why did I do
Why did you
Leave me again
Can't take this pain
You cast a spell on me
Then set me free
Not yours anymore
Lonely like before
I thought you were the one
Now you're gone
I have to accept
That we weren't meant

Dreams

I walk with you in my dreams
But nothing is as it seems
And as night falls you hear my screams

Because you hurt me before
When you walked out the door
Then came back to do it again
Causing me too much pain

So when I dream of you I cry
You made me want to die
And I still don't know why

You did this to me
I want to be free
From dreams of you
And heartache too

Me and You

It was meant to be me and you
Forever, but now we're through
Couldn't you see how much I cared
About you and all we shared

It's no longer me and you
Now I'm left feeling blue
What are you doing now
Do you miss me and how

I wanted it to be me and you
Didn't you want it too
How could you just leave
Now I'm left to grieve

RYL (recoveryourlife.com)

Since finding RYL
I've fell and I've fell
But each time you lifted me up again
Out of this sorrow and pain

You remind me there are others out there
Who also hurt, yet still care
Who respond each time
To this pain of mine
And remind me it's ok
That things will be better one day

Betrayal

You were my best friend
For many years
But you've found another
And left me in tears

She was my friend first
I introduced you both
Now I'm left alone
Like a lonesome goat

Watching you pal together
You now call me never
Unless one of you is away
You'll only call for me on that day

Now others have begun to talk
Asking why I'm alone on a walk
Even they say it's not fair on me
For I'm all alone, it's a tragedy

Feelings Aren't Facts

Feeling so lost, so blue
So many memories of you
I feel I'll never love again
Or ever get over this pain

I feel my life's a waste
I'm just a burden on this place
No one loves or cares for me
If I died they'd all be free

Feeling that I ate too much
And I'm too fat to be touched
These things seem so real to me
But feelings aren't facts, can't you see

That none of this is true
There's no reason to feel blue
There are many who will care
Waiting out there

Help

Feeling so awful
I just want to scream
Wish I could wake up
And find it's a dream
Wish I could kill myself
No one listens or helps
My head feels like it's going to explode
I can't cope with this load
But I mist go on as normal
It's expected of me
I'm not allowed fall apart
I'm not allowed break free
How many times must I attempt suicide
How many years must I starve myself
Before they'll listen
And offer me help

Normal

I want to recover
I don't want to be remembered this way
I could try to kill myself
But I'm not ready to give up
What this is doing to me is pathetic
I don't want to spend the rest of my life like this
I can't imagine being well
But I'd almost rather die
Than stay like this
I'm the only one who can make myself better
But I can't do it alone
They say I'm fading away
And I've almost collapsed
I just wanted to be thin
Now I want a normal life

Crimson Tears

Crimson tears flow
It's so hard to let go
But he's moved on
And now he's gone
Out of my life
I'll never be his wife
All that we shared
The only one who cared
Now he's no longer mine
I'm so sick of crying
Crimson tears
All these years

Hurt

Why do we let others hurt us
It doesn't seem fair
When it would be so much easier
Just not to care
But it's nice to feel loved
Though it hurts when they leave
And you're left behind to grieve

But know that not everyone is the same
They're not all playing games
And someday you will find the one
Who will love you as much as the rising sun

Control

I can't deal with life's problems
So I deal in my own way
By focusing on food and weight
When I don't feel great
Worrying about weight gain
Or causing myself physical pain
Takes my mind off what's going on
So I feel I can be strong

But I'm not strong at all
I'm only going to fall
Deeper into pain
If I do this again
But it's the only way to control
The pain inside my soul

Dear Cat

Oh cat of mine
Where are you?
You never stay out
All this time

I miss you
And I need you
Please come back
Before I crack

I know you like to roam
But please come home
You're needed here
I've shed many a tear

Since you've been gone
I try to carry on
But I miss you every day
Please come back to stay

Numb

I thought I felt sad
When I lost people before
But that doesn't even compare
To losing you
You were beside me every day
My friend in every way
Now I'm just numb
Don't know what to do
Can't even write or make a rhyme
Not this time
Nothing seems to matter anymore
But getting you back
When you return I'll hug you to death
My friend, my companion, my beloved pet

Die or Fly?

I sit here by the lake
I reflect on my mistakes
Should I choose to die
Or choose to fly

I could easily drown myself
Or go and ask for help
I stare at the water
And think it over

I don't want to leave my family
Because they would miss me
So I spread my wings and fly
Today I won't die

That Was Then

Tangled in your murderous web
Caught up in the lies you said
Engulfed by a wave of sadness
Lost in a night of darkness

I withdraw from all around
By turning in on myself
Until the light again I found
By asking for help

When it comes I flourish
My body and mind I nourish
With words and wisdom beyond my years
Which dry away all my tears

Happier Days

Depression and suffering
Are a part of my past
But I'll never forget them
As long as life lasts

For the scars remain
Long after the pain
But that's over now
I've moved on somehow

And found happier days
And healthier ways
To cope with life's downs
I have smiles instead of frowns

So I won't look back
Or go off track
For I have learned lessons well
I won't go back to that hell

I know I have the strength to survive
I'm happy now to be alive
For this is my chance
To sing and dance

Moving On

You used to be here in this place
Holding me in your loving embrace
I used to long for your kiss
Until I learned it was poisonous

Because one day
You went on your way
And broke my heart in two
You left me all blue

But now I've moved on
I am singing my song
Of freedom and peace
Away from all your grief

Love's Mistake

You say you love me
Yes you do
But you don't know
I'm no good for you

For when we kiss
I feel pleasure
Stirrings inside
I cannot measure

It's your blood I take
You made a mistake
When my love you hired
For I am a vampire!

Feelings of Happiness

Feelings of happiness
Explode inside me
Now I know for sure
This is the way to be

No more sadness
Or eating less
Than I should
No more letting of my own blood

Just spending time with loved ones
Doing things I enjoy
Like reading, singing and dancing
And minding a little baby boy!

For help or information on the issues in this book please go to:

www.recoveryourlife.com

www.pieta.ie

www.bodywhys.ie

www.dpselfhelp.com

Or email jo@samaritans.org

Author Bio:

Nicola Ward lives in Dublin, Ireland where she studied drama and dance.

She has a passion for music, musical theatre, singing, writing, and other creative arts.

She enjoys cuddling next to her cat and reading a great book during her spare time.

Hurt is her first poetry book.